Sesame Street® Self-Care

Yummy in My Tummy

Learn about Healthy Eating with Sesame Street

Charlotte Reed

Lerner Publications ◆ Minneapolis

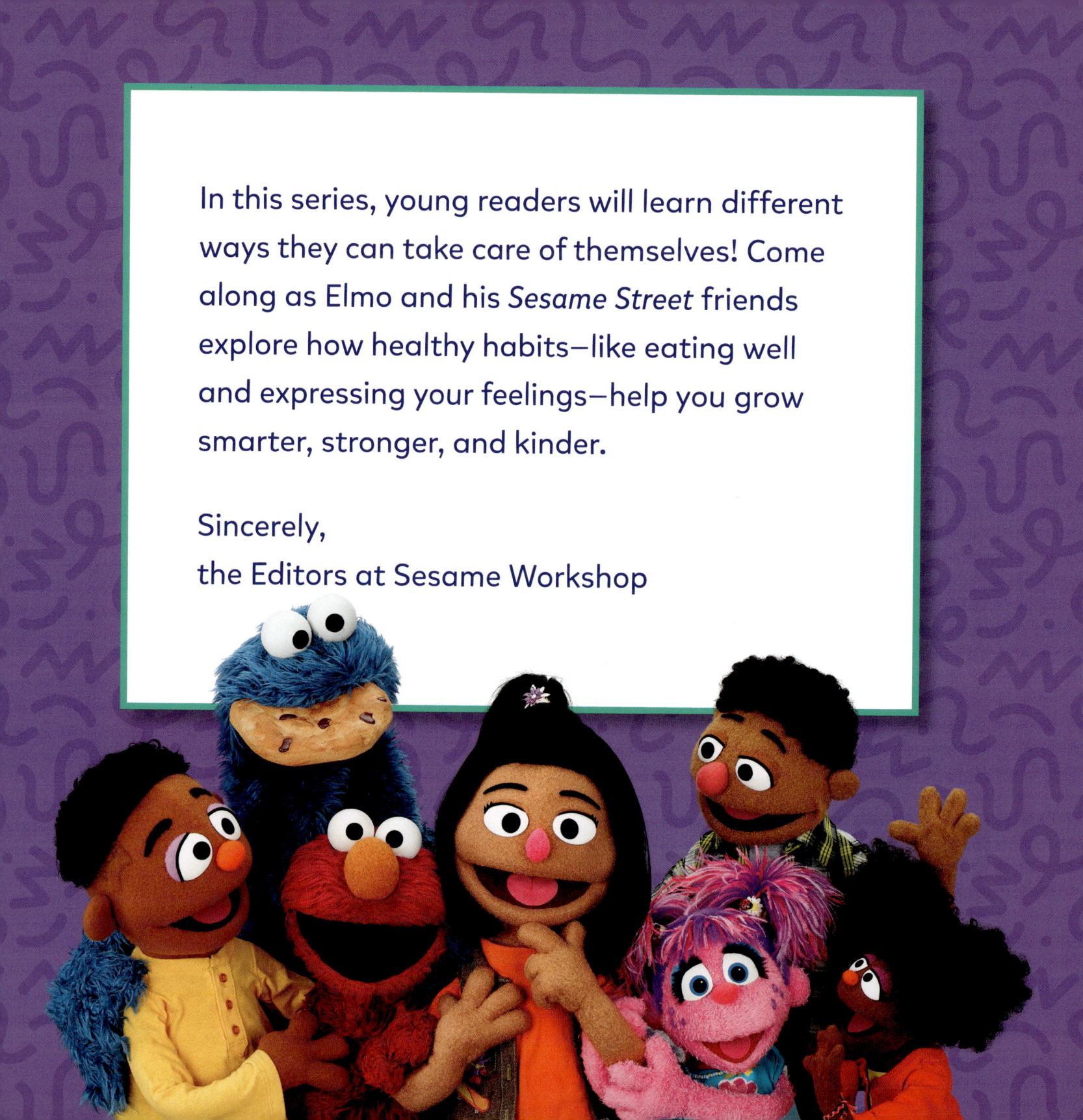

In this series, young readers will learn different ways they can take care of themselves! Come along as Elmo and his *Sesame Street* friends explore how healthy habits—like eating well and expressing your feelings—help you grow smarter, stronger, and kinder.

Sincerely,
the Editors at Sesame Workshop

Table of Contents

Healthy Eating 4

How to Eat Healthy 6

Healthy You! 21
Glossary 22
Read More . . . 23
Index 24

Healthy Eating

There are many things we do every day to take care of ourselves. One way we take care of ourselves is by eating healthy.

How to Eat Healthy

Eating healthy means eating foods that help keep your body strong.

Healthy eating keeps you super strong like me!

You can eat healthy by eating breakfast, lunch, dinner, and healthy snacks. Drinking water every day is important too!

When you're eating your healthy meals, look for the colors of the rainbow: red, orange, yellow, green, blue, indigo, and violet. Try to eat at least three colors, including green!

It's important to listen to your body. If you're hungry in between meals, have a healthy snack! If you're thirsty, drink some water!

Elmo loves to have watermelon as a snack!

Fruits, vegetables, grains, and proteins are good for you. You can help pick out these healthy foods at a store with your grown-up.

Cookies and cakes are sometimes foods. That means they're good to eat sometimes!

There are so many delicious things to eat! It's fun to try new foods. Try taking at least two bites of any new food!

Eating healthy foods gives us energy so we can grow, play, and learn every day!

What's your favorite food?

Healthy You!

You can have a healthy snack between meals! There are many to choose from. You can have a fruit smoothie, vegetables with dip, or a fresh fruit ice pop.

Glossary

cakes: baked foods made from a sweet batter or dough

grains: foods such as wheat, rice, and oats

oatmeal: a hot cereal boiled in water or milk

plate: a dish from which food is eaten or served

Read More

An, Priscilla. *Mindfulness While Eating.* Parker, CO: Child's World, 2023.

Bureau, Vicky. *Eat Healthy Foods.* New York: Crabtree, 2024.

Cook, Jennifer. *Grow Your Colors: Planting and Eating Healthy Foods with Sesame Street.* Minneapolis: Lerner Publications, 2024.

Photo Acknowledgments

Image credits: bigacis/Shutterstock, p. 3 (cereal); Drazen Zigic/Getty Images, p. 4; Valerii Apetroaiei/Getty Images, p. 7; Gorynvd/Shutterstock, p. 8; Prostock-Studio/Getty Images, p. 10; Valery121283/Shutterstock, p. 11 (broccoli); Cultura RM Exclusive/Frank and Helena/Getty Images, p. 13; Aleksandar Jankovic/Getty Images, p. 14; JGI/Jamie Grill/Getty Images, p. 16; Tetra Images/Getty Images, p. 18; SolStock/Getty Images, p. 20.

Design element: Dedraw Studio/Shutterstock.

Index

breakfast, 8–9

dinner, 8

lunch, 8

rainbow, 10

water, 8, 12

For my friends Leela and Leah for the food and laughter we've shared

Sesame Street® and associated characters, trademarks and design elements are owned and licensed by Sesame Workshop. © 2025 Sesame Workshop. All rights reserved.

International copyright secured. No part of this book may be reproduced, stored in a retrieval system, or transmitted in any form or by any means—electronic, mechanical, photocopying, recording, or otherwise—without the prior written permission of Lerner Publishing Group, Inc., except for the inclusion of brief quotations in an acknowledged review.

Lerner Publications Company
An imprint of Lerner Publishing Group, Inc.
241 First Avenue North
Minneapolis, MN 55401 USA

For reading levels and more information, look up this title at www.lernerbooks.com.

Main body text set in Mikado. Typeface provided by HVD.

Editor: Annie Zheng **Designer:** Laura Otto Rinne

Library of Congress Cataloging-in-Publication Data

Names: Reed, Charlotte, 1997- author.
Title: Yummy in my tummy : learn about healthy eating with Sesame Street / Charlotte Reed.
Description: Minneapolis : Lerner Publications, [2025] | Series: Sesame Street self-care | Includes bibliographical references and index. | Audience: Ages 4-8 | Audience: Grades K-1 | Summary: "Eating healthy helps keep your mind and body strong. Learn fun ways to fill your plate with healthful foods and how to keep your energy up to grow, play, and learn every day"— Provided by publisher.
Identifiers: LCCN 2024006499 (print) | LCCN 2024006500 (ebook) | ISBN 9798765643693 (library binding) | ISBN 9798765658116 (epub)
Subjects: LCSH: Nutrition—Juvenile literature. | Health—Juvenile literature.
Classification: LCC RA784 .R438 2025 (print) | LCC RA784 (ebook) | DDC 613.2—dc23/eng/20240412

LC record available at https://lccn.loc.gov/2024006499
LC ebook record available at https://lccn.loc.gov/2024006500

ISBN 979-8-7656-6239-7 (pbk.)

Manufactured in the United States of America
1-1010918-52410-7/12/2024